BETWEEN THE DREAMING

AND THE COMING TRUE

BETWEEN THE DREAMING
AND THE COMING TRUE

The Road

Home

to God

—⊸∞∞⊷—

Robert Benson

HarperSanFrancisco
An Imprint of HarperCollins*Publishers*

HarperCollins Web Site: http://www.harpercollins.com

HarperCollins®, 👜®, and HarperSanFrancisco™ are trademarks of HarperCollins Publishers Inc.

FIRST EDITION

Library of Congress Cataloging-in-Publication Data
Benson, R. (Robert)
  Between the dreaming and the coming true : the
  road home to God / Robert Benson.—1st ed.
      p.   cm.
  ISBN 0—06—060973—7 (cloth)
  ISBN 0—06—060900—1 (pbk.)
  1. Spiritual life–Christianity. 2. Desire for God.
  3. Benson, R. (Robert). I. Title.
BV4501.2.B395 1996
248.8'6—dc20   96—14554

96 97 98 99 00 ❖ HAD 10 9 8 7 6 5 4 3 2 1

This book is for
Alan, Barbara, Leigh, Jill, John, and Russell—
without whom there might well be no writer.

And it is for
Sara and Cindy—
without whom there would be no book.

And it is for
all the Friends of Silence & of the Poor—
without whom there may be no hope.

BETWEEN THE DREAMING

AND THE COMING TRUE

Beginning

---❧---

I would almost rather we had died that day
than to have found ourselves here,
lost somewhere between the dreaming
and the coming true.

Samuel to Constance
Samuel's Suite, 1976

In a class that I was in once, I saw a man with his well-worn, heavily marked Bible open before him, playing a game of "trap the teacher." He should have known better than to try to trap this particular teacher. Those who pray the Psalms by heart do not rattle very easily.

The teacher was finishing up a series of talks on praying the Psalms that she had been giving to a community of about sixty of us. I do not now remember the man's question. I remember only that it had a "Well, that is all very well and good, but the God of Abraham [and, therefore, of judgment and vengeance, one got the feeling] is going to make sure that the good guys get into heaven and the bad guys don't, no matter what" edge to it. It was asked in a spirit that was not exactly in keeping with the spirit of our prayer community, which was to be together for two years.

Hazelyn McComas looked at him for a minute and then said softly, and with fire in her eyes, "I cannot answer that. But I can say this: We Christians are awfully hard on each other and on ourselves, too. And we seem to be especially that way about things that may not really matter."

She is a kind and gentle woman, a teacher, a woman of prayer, a woman whose spirit bears witness to her having spent a life seeking for glimpses of and listening for whispers of God within the ancient prayer of the Chosen People. I remember that she drew a breath and straightened up a bit, as though she wanted to be firm and clear, but not harsh and critical.

"This is what I believe: We were with God in the beginning. I do not understand that exactly—what we looked like, what we did all day, how we got along, any of it. Then we were sent here. And I am not sure that I understand that very well, either. And I believe that we are going home to God someday, and what that will be like is as much a mystery to me as any of the rest of it.

"But I believe those things are true and that what we have here on earth in between is a longing—for the God that we have known and for the God that we are going home to."

———⚮———

God has always known us, it seems. The poet of Psalm 139 thought so: ". . . my body was no mystery to you, when I was formed in secret, woven together in the depths of the earth. Your eyes foresaw all my deeds, and they were all recorded in your book; my life was fashioned before it had come into being."

Jesus spoke of it, too. On the night he gathered with his friends for the last supper they would have together before he walked into the night and into the day when he would begin the climb up the hill to the cross, he seemed to be speaking to his friends as plainly as he could about the things he wanted them to remember. "You did not choose me, I chose you," he said to those gathered around the table, and to all of us who have come after them. That we are known and chosen is something God thought was important enough to send a Son to tell us.

In a letter written from a prison cell, where presumably one is careful to say only what one thinks is very important, Paul reminded his friends in Ephesus that "God chose us before the world was founded."

Whether one is drawn by the prayer of the poet or the words of the Christ or the words of the imprisoned preacher, the message is clear. God has always known us, and has chosen us even, in spite of everything, including ourselves.

Our being known by God does not begin when we first recognize it or when we acknowledge it or even when we make our first struggling attempts to come to grips with what it might mean for the creator of the universe to know us and choose us. It begins at the beginning, when we are first imagined into being.

⸻

"There is a Dream dreaming us," said an African Bushman to Laurens Van der Post.

One assumes that the Dreamer is the same one who looked at the darkness and said, "Let there be light." The same Dreamer delighted enough in that one act to choose to let there be light every twenty-four hours ever since, as though he cannot get enough of it himself. Can it be that the One who imagined the sun rising over the dark edges of the world each day imagined me in the Dreamer's own image in my own place?

"Imagine that," I hear someone's old aunt say in wonder. "Yes," says the one who prays the Psalms. "Yes," says the trap-the-teacher man. "Yes," says the Story.

Do God's dreams come true? say I.

⸎

Why didn't God just keep us, instead of sending us here to wander through all of this stuff we call our lives? Would God really run the risk of some of us not making it home again? What is the object of the exercise here, and what are our lives about? Selfish creature that I am, what am I supposed to be about while I am here?

"I do not know even now what it was that I was waiting to see," says a character in one of Eudora Welty's stories, "but in those days I was convinced that I saw it at almost every turn." I too have been looking, waiting all my life to see something I am not sure I will recognize, but know for certain is there. "You are traveling a new road with which you are very familiar," a friend once said to me at a critical juncture in my life.

I need to see why it is that we are here to see anything at all. I have caught only fleeting glimpses of it from time to time—as through a glass darkly, one might say—no matter how fiercely I watch. I hear a rustling behind me or a whisper on the wind, detect a smile or a gesture between friends or lovers or strangers, touch a stone or a blossom or the hand of my children—and it is there. I watch and listen with a fierceness reserved only for this search.

When I was younger, I worried a good deal about whether or not I was going to make it home to God. I was never quite convinced that those who interpreted the Story in the way that the trap-the-teacher man did were right, but I met enough of them to be more than a little afraid.

What I fear now is that I will somehow miss what it is that I am supposed to learn here, something important enough that the Dreamer dispatched me, and the rest of us, here to learn. What I fear now is that I will somehow miss the point of living here at all, living here between the dreaming and the coming true.

One

---⚬⚬⚬---

We praise you with joy, loving God,
for your grace is better than life itself.
You have sustained us through the darkness,
and you have blessed us with life
in this new day.

The Psalm Prayer at Morning Prayers
The Upper Room Worship Book

ON A FINE SPRING DAY not too many years ago, I had been given about two weeks to live, give or take the amount of time it would take me to successfully accomplish the technique that I decided to use to commit suicide. One cannot pass such a milestone each new year without a certain amount of reflection.

That spring, I spent an afternoon with my head in my hands, sitting cross-legged on the floor in my house, while a friend sat next to me and convinced me that I could raise my hand and ask for help without killing myself.

That spring, I spent an evening having dinner with my sister, telling her that I was going to go see Russell—"He always knows what to do"—and asking her if she would go with me to help me tell the story without breaking down. "I will pick you up at eight in the morning," I told her, and went home to cry and sleep.

That spring, thinking that it might well be a long time before I could do so again, I took a long walk down one of my favorite streets as I headed toward the hospital to see the doctor that Russell had arranged for me to see. I do not remember the doctor's name. I do remember that after an hour or so he said to me, "Would you like to stay with us here for a while, where it is safe?"

That spring, I spent a long hour waiting for someone to come from another part of the hospital to take me to the floor where I was going to stay. My sister waited with me, holding my hand, breathing a sigh of relief each time I returned from the smoking bench outside, as though she had not really believed me when I had said I would be right back.

That was the spring that I met Norma.

The elevator bell rang and the door opened, and there she was. She looked down at me and said my name with a question mark at the end, and I stood up and she took me across to the other side of the hospital. I held my sister's hand as we followed Norma, who chatted cheerfully the whole way. I was afraid of her right from the start.

———— ✕✕✕ ————

Though the risk of melodrama is high, I need to tell you something more of the state I was in during the weeks and months before I followed Norma through the maze of the hospital corridors and passageways. Those of you who have ever made such a journey will recognize some of your own story in mine; those who have not made such a visit to the edge may find some orientation helpful. I could not name it yet, but I was suffering from what William James called "a positive and active anguish, a sort of psychical neuralgia wholly unknown to normal life."

For the previous ten or twelve years, I had made my living as a copywriter and editor—a professional wordsmith, if you will. My work pattern had always been that I would work at the computer keyboard for an hour and a half to two hours and then take a few minutes to recharge myself. I would take a walk or make phone calls or go down the hall to check with somebody about something that needed to be checked on. Armed with a fresh cup of coffee, I would sit down for another "turn," as I called it. Two to four turns a day was a day's work, depending on my workload for the week. During the last few months, my turns had begun to reshape themselves based on my declining capacity to concentrate. At the end, a turn was six to fifteen minutes in front of the computer screen and an hour or so of wandering around to get my mind clear enough to work again. My office was near a college campus, and I used to find myself wandering through the campus, not ever being quite certain how long I had been there. By the time I followed Norma across the hospital, I could scarcely write a sentence. And I was scared to death.

I thought I was losing my mind, and it turns out that I was not too far off the mark. On the morning that I was to pick up my sister to go see Russell, I ran two red lights in a row without even seeing them until I had passed them by. I was too afraid to cross the major intersection that stood between her house and mine, and so I ended up going to town without her. When Norma came to take me away, I figured that I was being taken away for good, that I was likely to spend the rest of my life in a padded room trying to make sense of the task of tying my shoes. Later in the day, they came and took my shoestrings away from me, along with my belt, my pocketknife, my car keys, and my shoes. I remember being relieved. They were afraid I might hurt myself with them; I was afraid I would never be able to figure out which of the three drawers in my room to put them in.

Other than having a vague notion that what was happening to me was somehow connected to stress, I did not have a clue as to what was wrong with me. I knew only that my mind had gone bad for some reason, that I was incapable of working or coping, that I felt paralyzed and incapable of making even the simplest decisions, and that I was afraid of both living and dying.

So with one hand in my pocket and the other in my sister's hand, I followed Norma. I did it because it seemed to be literally the only thing that I could do.

———✸———

Norma led me to a small office that was just large enough for a desk, a tall filing cabinet, two chairs— and turning around, if there were no more than two people in the room. The walls had a ridiculously cheerful yellow wall covering, and the door had a window so that you could watch people go by in the hall. And people could see you as they went by. I was not watching the parade, however. I was busy watching the walls close in around me.

Norma said, "I will be back in a few minutes to do an intake interview with you. It will only take about ten or fifteen minutes to do that and then we can decide if you want to stay with us for a few days. You just relax here for a bit."

"Sure," I said, as though relaxation were possible.

I spent about two hours in that room. Norma would come and ask me a few questions and write down the answers, and then I would get anxious and ask, or tell, her to leave and she would go away for a bit. My sister alternated between coming in to hold my hand and looking nervously through the glass while Norma asked her questions. They both wanted to be in there, but I could not stand the crowd.

Finally I told Norma that I would like to go home and think about whether or not I wanted to stay. She came and stood about two feet from me. She was taller than me by a good four or five inches, and she

looked down into my face and back into my eyes
somewhere and smiled very firmly. "You are too sick
to go anywhere. You cannot leave now. You do not
have to stay forever, but you do have to stay the rest
of the day and tonight. Tomorrow, we will see what
happens."

"I do not want to," I said.

She ignored me. "Your sister will come in and get
a list of things you need from home and who you
want called, and I will go arrange for a room where
you can lie down and rest for a bit." She opened the
door and my sister came in.

"I decided that I'll stay overnight," I said, as though
I had actually decided the issue. I had been right about
Norma from the beginning; I was right to be afraid.
She had a good deal more in mind for me than a nap
and a meal and a good night's rest.

My sister made notes while I told her the calls
that had to be made and the things that had to be
taken care of. When we finished, Norma handed me
a paper to sign, showed me to my room, gave me a
sedative, and told me to lie down. I fell asleep almost
immediately, and slept for hours.

When I woke up, Norma was in the room.
"Thank you for letting me stay," I managed.

With a grin, she said, "I am glad that you decided
to. You are very sick, and you would have hurt yourself."

———∞———

That was on Tuesday. On Friday morning, after a series of long conversations with a small army of smil-
ing folks in white jackets ("Can you tell us a little bit
about why you are here?" they invariably began), a
battery of tests (with inkblots and black-and-white
photographs and round pegs and square holes and
everything), and one long, frightening night spent
reading William Styron's *Darkness Visible,* his memoir
about his struggles with depression ("Are you sure
this is a good time for you to read this?" asked the
friend I had asked to go out and buy it for me), I
awoke early in the morning to a world that was very
different from the one I had lived in most of my life.

It was Good Friday, the day when Jesus would be
killed again, the day when the cross would be draped
in black and carried in silence from the sanctuary
while those in the pews came face-to-face with the

hopelessness of a world in which the Light has been extinguished.

It was also my birthday, and the celebration would consist of a brief comment by one of the staff members at the morning gathering of patients and staff—it seemed as though he was saying, "This is Robert's birthday, and we need to be careful that he doesn't get too emotional—a surprised "Oh, it's your birthday" from my doctor when he made the rounds, and a ten-minute visit in the lobby with my sister and brother and nephew while a nurse watched us on a security monitor to be sure there was no knife in the cake and that I did not make a dash for the elevator.

I was soon to be divorced again and alone. I had lost my home and my daily life with my two young children. I was trying to make it in a job that did not fit me very well. I was unable to write a sentence, and all of the professional dreams I had ever had had gone down in failure, mismanagement, or bankruptcy.

And I was in a hospital room on a psychiatric ward, surrounded by people whose lives were a shambles, being tended to by strangers who were displaying the severest of mercies I had ever known. My window

looked out on a billboard from a car company that
had rigged the sign with lights so that whenever I
woke in the night I was staring at two giant brake
lights that flashed on and off all night.

And I was sick, sick enough to die. In fact, I had
been sick for years and had not known it. "Thus depression, when it finally came to me," wrote Styron,
"was no stranger, not even a visitor totally unan-
nounced; it had been tapping at my door for decades."

Clinical depression takes years to develop in most
cases, twenty-seven in mine, and it will take me years
to recover from it. I will not trouble you, or myself,
with all of the details involved in that recovery. Ex-
cept to say that in the company of my psychiatrist,
two social workers, psychologist, charge nurse, three
shift nurses, therapy group, recreational therapist,
three friends who came for visits and conversations
and confessions, a minister who came each week to
bring me the Eucharist, and the eleven people on the
ward who were just as sick as I was, my life was taken
apart, story by story, relationship by relationship, fear
by fear. On this day I am not completely well, but I
do know how I got sick, and I do have some idea of
what it takes to be healed.

None of which would have happened had it not been for Norma.

⸺ ∞ ⸺

One cannot read the stories of Jesus without coming face-to-face with the healing stories. And one cannot help but feel a bit queasy when one reads them. After all, in the way they are presented in the Gospels, and very often in the way they are preached to us, one can get the sense that such healing events are a function of the faith of the healed. That if we, in fact, had more faith, we could command more such miracles in our day, that the Christ would touch and heal us too if only we had the faith and devotion and spirit of those who lived and walked in the Middle East two thousand years ago. Those who believe that may be right; I cannot argue with them.

But the other thing one can see in those same stories is that a fair number of those whom Jesus healed were delivered, some kicking and screaming, into the presence of Jesus. And it is there that many of us find ourselves and our own stories.

In *Brendan*, Frederick Buechner's novel about a sixteenth-century Irish saint, there is a scene in which a crippled, bitter old priest named Gildas falls to the floor during an argument with a discouraged Brendan while one of Brendan's followers looks on and tells the story.

> "I am as crippled as the dark world," Gildas says.
>
> "If it comes to that, which one of us isn't, my dear?" Brendan replies.
>
> Gildas with but one leg. Brendan sure he's misspent his whole life entirely. I who had left my wife to follow him and buried our only boy. The truth of what Brendan said stopped all our mouths. We was cripples all of us . . . .
>
> "To lend each other a hand when we're falling," Brendan said. "Perhaps that's the only work that matters in the end."

In the dark days when the Christ came to me as I lay there on my mat in the glare of the brake lights— or was it in the dust, begging alms at the city gate, or beside the pool whose waters promised healing if only I could reach them in time, or along the road where one could make mud for the eyes from spittle and dirt, or on the road to Mary and Martha's house,

where the crowd jockeyed for position and a good
seat, or in the tomb with Lazarus himself, wrapped
in bandages, beginning to rot, alone in the dark—on
the day when Christ said to me, "Do you want to be
healed?" it was Norma who kept saying yes, not me.
I was too tired, too ill, too afraid, too uncertain, too
ready to die. It was Norma and my sister and my
friends and a couple of dozen strangers who took me
to the Healer.

"Your faith has made you whole," said Jesus to one
he had healed. In fact, in many cases it was the faith
of those who came running through the town to tell
the cripple that the Healer was nearby and convinced
him that it was worth the effort to try and get there.
It was the faith of those who carried the litter, pushed
through the crowd, tore off the roof tiles, lifted the
litter, struggled across the roof in the sun, lowered
the rope, and ran downstairs to tell Jesus that the
man who was coming through the roof was ready to
be healed, whether the man knew it or not. It was
their faith, or hope or desire or concern or wild dream
or crazy idea, or something. In the end, it was their
love for the cripple that made him whole.

———— ∞ ————

I have not seen Norma for a very long time. Sometimes I happen to be driving by the hospital about the time when the day nurses are headed across the street to the parking lot, and I recognize some of them and I smile. Once when I was visiting a friend in another part of the hospital, I ran into one of the social workers, but he was busy escorting someone else, someone else whose time it was to be lowered through the roof, and so I did not stop him to talk. I wonder about all of them, though, and I wonder if they have any idea of what it is they do up there on that ward with the locked doors and the art therapy and the white coats and the barefoot patients, if they have come to see it for the work that it really is.

On the day that it was time for me to leave the hospital, I stood in the hallway beside the nurse's station, my things on a metal cart, my sister waiting downstairs in the car to take me home. I was waiting for Norma to tell me what to do. I stood there for a while and she finally appeared, and saw the question in my eyes.

"Pick up your stuff and go," she said. Her smile gave no trace of whether or not she knew that what she had said was the same thing that Christ had said when he had sent another man home, his things under his arm, a bounce in his step, and a wonder in his heart at the love of those whose faith had made him whole.

Two

God said, "Let there be light,"
and there was light.
And God saw that the light was good.
This very day the Lord has acted,
may God's name be praised.

The Versicle at Morning Prayer
The Upper Room Worship Book

In the beginning, God created the heavens and the earth and the light and stars and animals and what must have been some wondrous garden and, of course, humans. But we had no sooner finished up our first big assignment, naming the chimpanzees and kangaroos and so forth, and begun to wonder a good bit about the kind of fun that the two different kinds of humans might have together when the sun went down, when we stumbled upon the tree with what seemed to be the best fruit. The next thing we know, God is handing us clothes thrown together from animal skins and showing us to the gate. A mere eighty verses into the story of the relationship between God and the ones created in the divine image, and there we are in the darkness outside the garden, dressed like refugees from a creation-day dress rehearsal, trying to fend for ourselves, and without a mall in sight.

According to the Story, the pace of the good-bye business picks up from there. Cain says good-bye to Abel. Noah says good-bye to his neighbors, all of them, from the deck of the boat that would save them if he would let them on board. Lot says good-bye to Sodom and Gomorrah and his wife. Jacob says good-bye (and "Gotcha") to his brother. Joseph says good-bye from the bottom of a pit to his best jacket and his brothers. Moses says good-bye to the promised land after only a glimpse of it after all those years in the desert. Judah says good-bye to Israel and Israel says good-bye to Jerusalem. Elijah takes his leave without leaving so much as a note or a grave or even a body behind.

Skip ahead a few hundred pages; it does not get any better. John the Baptist says good-bye to his newly won converts—and his head, for that matter. Mary barely has time to open the shower gifts and she is off to Egypt in the middle of the night, with a husband she has never slept with and a baby who draws a crowd of kings and angels and shepherds wherever he goes, and without a mother-in-law to watch the kid while she recovers. Simeon's reward is to say good-bye as soon as he says hello to the Child for whom he has been waiting all these years.

Jesus himself started saying good-bye almost as soon as he arrived. There was a strange and irritated fare-thee-well to his family—one that he would not even come to the door and say to them face-to-face: "Who is my mother? Who are my brothers?" Later there was an almost unnoticed one said to Judas at the supper table, and one to his Father in the garden, a prayerful good-bye that caused him to sweat blood. And there was an angry, anguished one from the cross.

The disciples say good-bye to Jesus without knowing what they are saying. By the time he turns up on the road to Emmaus, he is forgoing even saying good-bye; he just disappears when people look up from the dinner table. Finally he says good-bye without a trace from the top of an unidentified hill that has somehow managed to become the object of a holy war ever since.

For a journey home to God and to each other and to our own sweet selves, this road we travel seems to have more than its share of good-byes.

There must be something in all of this good-bye
business for us to know. There must be something
that God wants to tell us in the last place, something
that can be said only after we have said good-bye in
the first place.

⚬⚬⚬

Saint John's telling of the Story begins with the word
that in the beginning the Word that was with God
was Jesus and that Jesus was sent here to be with us.
Theories as to the real reason Jesus was sent begin to
multiply pretty rapidly after that. Some of them are
offered up by Jesus himself.

"I am come that you might have life," he says to
some.

To others he says, "Do not think that I have come
to bring peace; I have come to bring a sword."

"I have come so that you might know the Father,"
he says to his friends on the last night, or what they
all thought was the last night—and was, in a way.

Could Jesus have come so that he might know the
Father as well? One may well have been with God in
the beginning, one may recognize God's voice more

readily, one may well have more love or trust or courage or insight or faith than the rest of us, but could
it be true that there is something one cannot learn
about God as long as one is with God? People who
have nothing to learn about God do not sweat blood
at the prospect of saying good-bye to their friends.

———— ∞ ————

Deep within each of us is the urge to know and to be
known. It is as central to the core of our being as is
the urge to dance in the sunshine or cry at weddings
or sing in the shower or laugh at children or fall
backward into the snow. It is buried as deeply within
us as is the sense that it takes for us to know not to
give our children stones and serpents instead of bread
and fish. It is as much a part of us as hugging a child
or tending the sick or walking on the beach.

When we were given the capacity to love, to speak,
to decide, to dream, to hope and create and suffer, we
were also given the longing to be known by the One
who most wants to be completely known. It is a longing woven into the very fabric of the image in which
we were made.

My father fought cancer of one sort or another for fourteen years. When he was in the hospital for the last time, he spent a fair amount of those few weeks saying good-bye to people. Friends and business associates, brothers and sisters, children and grandchildren all came to say good-bye. Some of them came from out of town and called ahead to make sure it was okay to come; they did not want to show up at a bad time. Others had to be tracked down because they had not heard the news and my father wanted to be sure that he spoke to them before he went. Some of the ones who lived in town would come by for a visit and everyone else would be gone off to have a sandwich or a coffee or a good cry and suddenly it was just them and my dad and it would be their turn to say good-bye and have it said to them.

One afternoon, after some of his friends had just left—friends he well knew he would never see again—my father said to me, "I sure do hate saying good-bye." He squeezed my hand.

Without thinking, which likely accounts for whatever wisdom there is in the remark, I squeezed back and said, "But if you do not say good-bye, then you cannot say what comes next. And what comes next is always hello."

⊗⊗⊗

One of the consequences of having been sick enough to die once myself is that I am now much more interested in any celebrations regarding being raised from the dead than I once was.

For some years, I prepared for Easter by attending a Good Friday service and watching the cross go out the back door, its ominous and unsettling black veil flowing in the breeze, trying to summon up the courage to imagine and to face some semblance of the sense of loss the disciples must have felt on that day, trying to come to grips with what it means if there is another word after *good-bye* and what it means if there is not. Being close to being draped in black and carried out the same door myself has, shall we say, made the whole thing a bit easier for me to imagine.

I was in the hospital around Easter, and the doctors gave me a pass to go to church on Easter morning. My sister came to pick me up and help me get

37

there. Sitting in the pew that morning, barely two blocks from the hospital where I was told I might well have been dead instead of alive on this Easter morning, it came to me that resurrection is a theological concept that may well be ignored unless one's death cannot be.

It then follows that forgiveness is not much of a concept without something for which to forgive and be forgiven. Healing has no meaning in the absence of illness. Peace is no treasure at all to those who have known no war and no strife. Saying hello has no joy in it without the saying of good-bye.

I am coming to believe that the thing God said just before "Let there be light" was "Good-bye, dark." And that Noah could not say hello to the rainbow without first having said good-bye to the world as it disappeared beneath the waters of the flood. And that something deep and mysterious about saying good-bye from the bottom of a pit made the hello that Joseph spoke to his father all those years later all the more wondrous. "Good-bye, Egypt" turned out to be another way for the Israelites to say "Hello, Canaan."

"Good-bye, Jesus of Nazareth," whispers Mary through her tears at the foot of the cross on Friday afternoon. "Hello, Lord of the Universe," she murmurs to the one she mistakes for a gardener, on Sunday morning.

—⁂—

Even Jesus himself, the Word that was with God in the beginning, could not completely know the Father's love without leaving home. Until he came among us, God's good-bye ringing in his ears, Jesus could not know anything of providence or mercy or forgiveness or grace; he could not know the side of God that can be known only by those who have been away. He could not know what it was like to be missed, to be loved from afar, to be whispered to in the darkness of the wilderness or the garden or the tomb. He could not know what it means to recognize God's face in the sunrise or pray God's name into the glittering silence of the sky on a sweet summer night. He could not know what it means to see God in the face of a child or hear God in the rustle of the trees.

If in heaven there is no sin, no sickness, no pain, no suffering, then there is no mercy, either. And no compassion, no healing, no grace. There are no re-unions, no fathers running down the road toward children who have been away, no neighbors crowd-ing around to celebrate the finding of a lamb that has just come home on the shoulders of the shepherd. Who can blame God for wanting us to know these things about the One who dreamed us into being?

Until there is good-bye, there is no hello. Until there is a journey away, there is no coming home.

Three

Let us kneel before the Lord who made us.
For you are our God and we are your people,
we are the flock that you shepherd.
We will know your power and presence this day
if we will but listen for your voice.

Venite exultemus
From Psalm 95

I KNOW A LITTLE GIRL who claims that she talks with God and that God talks back. She is not the only little one who has ever made such a claim, but she is the only one who has made such a claim around me, so I listen to her. I am afraid not to.

I have a friend who used to wonder about basketball players who make the sign of the cross just before they shoot foul shots. He said that he was never sure that it made any difference but all the same he hated it when it was a guy on the other team who did it, especially during the last few seconds of a close game. "You never know," he would say.

That is pretty much the same logic I apply when it comes to my little friend and her claims. You never know.

If the Bible is to be believed on any sort of basis at all, then God has certainly done stranger things than talk to five-year-old girls.

━━━ ∞ ━━━

People whose view of the Scriptures is literal will tell you that they believe that God created the world in a few days, including kangaroos, trees that lose their leaves every year and some others that do not, broccoli and other assorted vegetables that masquerade as edible foods, and a couple of hundred different species of monkeys—the last presumably for pure entertainment value. According to these people, God was also responsible for whole armies being swallowed up by the sea, a whole person being swallowed up by a whale and spit back out at the appropriate moment, a whole nation being chosen for a seemingly endless cycle of blessing and exile and blessing and exile, and a whole crowd of folks being fed on a daily shower of whole bread from the sky.

They will tell you that God sent angels from heaven to visit various and sundry saintly and not-so-saintly folks, raised up prophets from among the

scared, the scurrilous, and the outcast, and made heroes out of an assorted group of unlikely folks. Moses
was a killer on the lam before he became the man
with the direct line to the Almighty. If Abraham had
slept with Sarah as much as he had his servant girl,
they might have had a family when they were young
enough to enjoy it. Jacob was a thief and a liar and a
pretty poor hunter to boot long before he was a central figure in the choosing of a people. David evidently
relaxed between psalm-writing sessions by spying on
his neighbor's wife while she took her bath; later on
he had the guy killed so she could take her baths at
his place and he would not have to walk up to the
roof to get a good look at her.

They will tell you that God impregnated a virgin
and convinced her betrothed it was okay, and sent
a son into the world whose opening demonstration
of his powers was the refilling of the wine jugs at a
three-day party. He then proceeded to hang out with
tax collectors and prostitutes and fishermen, throw
the finance committee out of the temple, and finally
die after obstinately stonewalling the local power
brokers, choosing to be murdered on their cross

rather than answer their questions. According to Christians, God sent a son to be misunderstood, betrayed, killed, and resurrected from the dead so that those of us who were with God in the first place could get back home to God in the last place.

The God that such a Story reveals is a God who does not seem limited in any way at all to normal, routine, everyday sorts of activities.

However, some of the same folks who will tell you those stories about God, and do so with a straight face and an earnest heart, will start to get nervous if you start talking about a God who talks to five-year-old girls in the late twentieth century. They will say it is cute of course that she thinks that, and then they will pat the child on the head as though they are certain that, in time, she will grow out of it.

I have some photographs of my daughter taken on a mountain-climbing expedition of sorts. She was two at the time, and had traveled halfway up a mountain in the snow and ice while riding on my back in a backpack before cooler, wiser heads prevailed and she was sent back to the bottom with her mother and grandmother and aunt, who were looking for a good reason to head back to the fireplace anyway. My father and sister and I finished the climb.

Two months later my father was in the hospital dying and I was showing him the photos from the climb. The photos showed the face of a little girl who was thrilled with the whole ordeal. And ready to climb anything, anywhere, anytime. One of the last things he ever said to me was a warning: "Don't let them get to her." He was afraid that if one were not careful, well-meaning grownups could well take from her the spirit that made her face shine that day in the dark cold of the mountain. And as time passed, they might take away the things a child loves most and believes the strongest and cannot explain.

Whenever I talk to people about five-year-olds who talk to God, I get the distinct impression that deep down they regard it as some sort of romantic foolishness, foolishness that the child will grow out of soon enough, even if I may well be a lost cause. As though burning bushes, eighty-year-olds making babies, and slingshots taking out giants from thirty paces were somehow indicative of God's aversion to anything out of the ordinary.

I say, you never know.

All of this talking-to-God business actually came into focus for me when another little friend that I have looked up at me one day and asked, "Do you know what happens to us when we die?" He had this look on his face that told me he knew the answer and that if I would resist the urge to pull some grown-up theological reasoning on him he would let me in on the secret. I waited for the answer and for him to finish his cookie.

"Well," he said, "God breaks us up into little pieces and takes the best parts of us and makes other people out of them."

This was a theory I had not heard before. I do not believe it, either. Reincarnation by component is an interesting idea, but it is not what caught my attention then or what holds it now. What he said next is what caught my attention.

"How do you know?" I asked offhandedly, reaching for a cookie of my own. Whatever the answer was going to be, I had a feeling that sustenance for the journey was a good idea.

"God told me. One night while I was asleep."

This pretty much confirmed what my first little friend had been trying to explain to me. She had told me once, "We really don't say things out loud to each other anymore, but I can hear him."

"You are sure it is him?" I had asked her. A question that earned me the "You may well be too dumb to be allowed to live" look often given to people of my advanced age. I have three children; I know the look.

"Does God like you?" I asked her a minute or so later.

She stifled a grin. She is a compassionate soul. "Yep," she said easily, confidently, certainly.

"How do you know?"

"Because of the way he talks to me. He just likes me. I recognize it in his voice."

The Voice that my little friends claim to hear and to recognize in the middle of the night is the same one that we grownups who call ourselves Christians claim to seek and to have found. It is the Voice that said, "Let there be light," and removed the darkness in a single sentence. It is the Voice that whispered the

Word that was in the beginning. It is the one that the Psalmist claims whispered us into being and the one that gives us counsel in the night.

It is not a voice to be trifled with. The Israelites heard it once and promptly demanded that from then on Moses take notes for them. We have pretty much been doing that one way or another ever since.

We love to read and tell the stories of the way that God spoke to Abraham, Moses, Samuel, David, Jonah, and the rest of them. However, we do not often re-mind ourselves that before they were heroes of the faith they were wanderers and wastrels, shepherds and stutterers, altar boys and mama's boys, small-time business folks and clumsy parents. Folks like us, pretty much. The difference is that they thought they heard the Voice and were foolish enough to say so and to act upon what they thought they heard.

We, however, claim that God speaks to us and then wait patiently in our pew for someone with a degree and a robe and a hospital parking pass to tell us what the Voice might be whispering to us deep inside. We pray for guidance and then worry about whether the voice we hear within is the Voice. We quote Saint Paul's admonition to work out own sal-

vation with fear and trembling, and then tremble at
the thought of acting on the counsel given to us in
our hearts in the night.

Perhaps we are afraid that God does not regard us
highly enough to speak to us anymore—a rather
funny position to take for those who claim to be the
children of God. Perhaps we are afraid that God no
longer speaks to anyone much anymore or that we
can no longer recognize the Voice. It could be that
we are afraid that God does still speak and that we
will hear and that the God of the publicans and sinners and scared and scurrilous will want to make
something new of us as well.

I am convinced that the Voice that whispered us
into being still whispers within us and all creation.
I am dead certain of it sometimes, terrified of it at
other times, longing for it at all times. The silence
that so often seems to overcome me is more likely a
matter of my not trusting my own ears than it is a
matter of the Voice having gone suddenly, inexplica-
bly silent.

Frederick Buechner has written that God speaks
to us all the time and that "if we were not blind as
bats, we could hear him." I am not certain about the

metaphor he uses, but I am certain of the truth he declares. We are closing our ears and then blaming God for the silence.

We had been traveling for a while, one of those seasons where you are home just long enough to repack and leave town again for a few days, and I was awakened one morning by the suddenly unfamiliar sounds of my own house. They were simple sounds, in their usual pattern, generally unnoticed and unremarked. I lay there in the darkness, trying to decide how quickly to move out of the bed and into the day, and suddenly the chorus began.

The coffeemaker switched on in the kitchen, and I heard the water bubbling its way up and into the basket and down into the pot. Old and heavy cats dropped to the floor in the room where they sleep, and then came the sound of their paws softly brushing on the door. My bare feet brushed across the hardwood floor, and the doorknob clicked as I opened it. The bedclothes rustled and the mattress squeaked as the lady I share this home with rolled over and snuggled down into the covers as I left the room.

I heard the first cup of coffee being stirred with a
tinkling sound. The sound of cars going by in the
semidarkness, carrying those whose livelihoods de-
pend on their arriving at some appointed place
hardly before the day has begun. The rustling of
pages in a book, the sound of a pen scratching back
and forth across a page I am trying to convert into a
reasonable facsimile of the story of yesterday's portion of my own journey. The chatter of birds at the
feeders that surround our house, chatter that re-
moves any doubt that God has let there be light and
this day is now to be entered into in full measure.

Later there is a set of sweet sighs and murmurs
and the first whispered greetings shared between me
and another in the Eden into which we have been
born this new day. Later there will be the clatter of
dishes and the zipping up of clothes and briefcases
and purses and coats. There will be snatches of conversation about yesterday and this afternoon and
what we are going to do a week from Thursday. And
the sound of a kiss and a little giggle and the closing
of a door and the sound of a car in the drive.

It is a three-hour symphony that is repeated
almost every day of my life. And when I will let it,

it reminds me that I am home, that I have a place, that a world that is mine to wander and wonder through has been created out of the darkness and the void and the deep once again.

The Reverend Buechner implores us to listen to our lives, to the very sound of them, for that is where, "if God speaks to us at all in this world . . . it is into our personal lives that he speaks." We need only listen to our own lives, I think, to hear the song of creation and compassion and companionship. It is in our lives that we can hear that there is a place for us among the many rooms of the Father's house. It is in our lives that we hear that God is with us still, and speaks even yet.

Somewhere in the silence, long ago, a Word began to be whispered out over the darkness and the deep. The sound of the stars gliding by, the creaking and groaning of the earth, the rush of the waters, the first clatter and calls and chatter of life followed soon thereafter.

And it happens each day again at my house, and yours. It is the symphony that follows the call to "Let there be light." It is the sound of the same Voice that whispered our names before we knew them ourselves, and whispers them still whether we listen or not. But when we do listen, we can begin to discover the sweet joys and graces and gifts that are to be found in a world that is being born again, and again and again.

———∞∞———

There is a story making the rounds right now about a four-year-old girl who was overheard whispering into her newborn baby brother's ear. "Baby," she whispers, "tell me what God sounds like. I am starting to forget."

Little children will lead us, of course, if for no other reason than that in this world of ours it may well be that it is only a little child who is capable anymore of hearing or recognizing or trusting the Voice that calls us. The rest of us may be too busy drowning out the Voice with calls and cries and shouts of our own. Or claiming ignorance when we should be claiming revelation.

All of which makes my little friends who talk to God more important to me than ever. Why should not one who was with God only five years ago—or five days ago, for that matter—be able to better recognize God's voice than one such as I, one whose memory of it as it whispered him into being has become so faded that it is an echo barely heard, if at all?

Four

Lord, you now have set your servant free,
to go in peace as you have promised.
For my eyes have seen the Light
that you prepared for all the world to see,
a Light to enlighten the whole world,
and to bring glory to your people.

Nunc dimittus
The Canticle of Simeon

I MET A LEAN, LEATHERY priest from Texas. He looked more like a rancher or a prospector than a priest. If he looked like a priest at all, it was Graham Greene's whiskey priest. Father Kelly's good Irish Catholic moniker notwithstanding, it was a lot easier to imagine him on a cattle drive to Laredo than on a pilgrimage to the Vatican.

At the time, he lived his life in a house of prayer along with two other priests and two nuns—the latter two being hermits with whom he speaks only once a year. He also spends a fair amount of time listening with the ever-changing gatherings of retreatants who come to the house in search of God.

To those of us who were listening to him that day, a crowd of us who fancied ourselves monks-in-the-making, and with an impish, surprising grin on his face, he issued a blanket invitation to come to Texas and see him sometime; he could arrange for all of the silence and solitude we could ever need. He said that if we did not want to, we would not even have to talk at lunch on Sundays, the hour each week that is set aside for conversation. A man who lives such a life, and who has also been a professor at a seminary, a missionary to the poor who live along the Mexican border, and a writer of deep and serious books on the work of Saint John of the Cross, is not a man to be taken lightly when it comes to theological discussion.

Among the other things he told us that day was that he was certain that in the end no one of us was ultimately going to be able to resist the love of God, that none of us was strong enough to keep ourselves from God. Which one of us, he asked, has behaved so miserably here that there is not enough love and mercy in God to warrant our forgiveness?

None of us knows what happens to us when we cross the last border, so to speak, and enter the world that only God has seen, the world that is home to the Dreamer. Are there any of us the Dreamer has dreamed into being that the Dreamer does not want to come true? Perhaps there is not enough forgiveness in heaven for liars and adulterers and cheats and murderers. Perhaps there is not enough for writers and other social misfits, either. But perhaps there is.

One of us who was listening asked Father Kelly what that sort of thinking did to his concept of heaven and hell. "Oh, I believe there is a hell all right," he said, flashing his grin again, as though he had heard this question before, and from some folks who were more theologically imposing than we were. "I just do not believe there is anyone in it."

———❦———

I spent a fair amount of time in church when I was growing up. For the first nine or ten years of my life, my father was a pastor in very small local churches. One of the churches had an apartment in the back where we lived. My brother and I had to be up and dressed for church on Sundays in time for my mother to make the beds and straighten up our room, because one of the Sunday school classes met there. Vacation Bible School was held in our kitchen during the summers. There is an old story we still tell at family gatherings about the time my younger brother and a buddy got thirsty during church one morning and wandered into the kitchen during a hymn that my father was leading and for which my mother was playing the piano. Without any grownups to suggest an alternative, the two four-year olds helped themselves to a little grape juice, conveniently left out on a tray in dozens of little cups on the kitchen table. My father made the discovery when he opened the lid of the tray that was to be passed through the aisles for communion a few minutes later.

I have never been told if there was a connection between that story and the fact that we moved to Nashville soon thereafter and my father went to work in the family's religious music publishing business. Technically that marked the end of my career as a preacher's kid, but it was not the end of my church-going.

Mondays and Tuesdays were pretty much ignored by the church when I was young, until somebody in denominational headquarters decreed that Monday night should be family night and put a bit more pressure on the family dinner table, a precursor of the concept of quality time, I suppose.

On Wednesdays there was the fellowship dinner
and prayer meeting and Bible study. On Thursdays,
when I was older, I went to the rehearsal for the
youth musical group in which my brother played
guitar and that my father led. On Saturdays I played
in the church basketball league. Sunday we went to
Sunday school, morning worship, and lunch, played
in the yard with church buddies, then went back to
church for rehearsal, youth group, and evening worship.

Two weekends a year we went on youth retreats;
one weekend a year we went on all-church retreats.
Because of the work that my father did, we went to
three major religious publishing conventions each
year, and from time to time we went downtown to
the War Memorial Auditorium for the All-Night
Gospel Singing. When I look back now, I wonder just
when I had time for sin.

But just in case I had, there were plenty of ser-
vices where the preacher led us in a couple of dozen
choruses of "Just As I Am" while rubbing his brow
and raising his hand and suggesting that he was willing to wait quite a while for someone to heed the call

and head for the altar. You learned to sit in the middle of the pew so that one of the older folks who roamed the aisles looking for the kind of pained expressions that could mean only that some major sin had been committed could not get you by the arm and whisper into your ear that they believed that the Lord was speaking to someone that night and they were pretty sure that it was you.

The two or three rows of teenagers in the back were, of course, pretty fertile territory for finding those who were ready to "start over for the Lord." Quarterly was about the average for some of us, a little more than that for those who were particularly sensitive or for those who got there late and had to sit on the ends of the pews. College students were on the twice-annual plan—summers and Christmas break.

The only kid I remember who went to the altar only once while he was in high school was Bill Griggs, the funniest teenager in our church. I have a theory that on the one night that Bill did go, God told him that eternity would be no fun without him, that he was a shoo-in and had nothing to worry about. He heard the word from God and never went back to the altar again that I recall.

Looking back, it seems as though an inordinate amount of time was spent preaching to the choir, as the saying goes, reminding us again and again that we were going to hell because we were not good enough to go home to God instead. I do not think that I am the only one who grew up there believing that the God of mercy was going to run out of forgiveness about the time my number came up.

I have a friend who grew up there with me. I remember seeing him at the altar on Sunday nights as much as I was there. He told me not too long ago that he did not even "really meet Christ" until his junior year in college. I have another friend who attended one of those churches where you got to spend Sunday night at home and watch *Bonanza* instead of going to church. Both of my friends are pastors now. It suggests to me that both Bill Griggs and Hoss Cartwright had some theological insight that I was not privy to.

Why is it that we in the church, the ones who claim to love people the most, are also the ones who have done the most to help people be afraid of the God we claim to know? Why do we so often preach the gospel as though it were a tool of punishment rather than an expression of love?

Like a fair number of folks who grew up around churches, I grew up feeling as though I had something to prove. And I always assumed that the one who had the doubts was God. The logical extension, of course, was that the primary activity to be undertaken here was to prove myself worthy enough to earn my passage through the pearly gates.

What were the odds that God—the one who dreamed me into being, whispered the breath of life into me, knit me together in my mother's womb, gifted me for a life that would bring glory and honor to God, and sent a Son to remind me that the plan was for me to come true and come home in the end—was going to throw it all away because I kissed a pretty cheerleader during the bus ride home from a high school basketball game when I was sixteen? The God who would do that has less mercy than your average well-intentioned local parent.

Yet that is what many of us were taught. And it is what many of us teach our children even now, even as we repeat the phrases about faith and works, as we remind them that we all have sinned and come up short somehow, as we sing two more choruses of "Jesus Paid It All."

The result is not a life of faith, but a life of fear. A result that does not lead to a life with God, but a life of avoiding God. It does not lead to a life in which we share the mercy and love and compassion of Christ, a life in which we spend our days breaking bread with other sinners or feeding people who have no food or helping to heal others' wounds or rejoicing in the good gifts we have been given by the Giver of all things. It more often leads to a life of anxiety and suspicion and hopelessness and self-centeredness, a life of starting over—over and over.

Perhaps that is why writer Eugene Petersen says, "It is important to go to church—I wouldn't think of not going—but you've got to be mature. It's not for beginners."

If this journey that we call our lives is some sort of test to see if we can behave well enough to go home to the One who made us, then we will fail, all of us. We cannot ever be good enough to deserve that; we are not even good enough to deserve the paradise to which we were sent.

The great risk is not that we will fail to qualify to be reunited with God. The risk is that we will somehow fail to understand why we are here. That we will end up believing that we are being punished because Adam and Eve were barking up the wrong tree. That we will be so fearful of the stories about separating the sheep from the goats that we will end up believing that it is okay to try to have God all to ourselves and shut out those who do not look, act, sound, believe, or worship the way we do. That we will see those stories as the only authentic God stories and put little faith in the ones about hungry prodigals and redeemed tax collectors and Johnny-come-lately yard workers and the lucky sinners brought in to fill up the banquet halls.

We are not here to show something to God. We are here because God—the One who wants to be completely known—has something to show to us.

Five

Lord, you have examined me and know me.
You know everything about me.
You are familiar with all my paths.
You have kept close watch over me.
Such knowledge is beyond my understanding.
Examine me and know my thoughts,
test me and understand my fears.
Guide me in the ancient and
everlasting ways.

Domine, probasti
From Psalm 139

I HAVE A PRIVATE THEORY that mothers have been genetically blessed when it comes to singing camp songs. So when I am alone in the car with my two young children, we very often play a game called When I Grow Up I Am Gonna Be _____. It is exactly the kind of Winnie-the-Pooh sort of game that a camp-song-challenged father would make up to pass the time when a six-year-old daughter and a four-year-old son are getting restless.

The rules of the game are simple. On the first round, you go from player to player, each one declaring what they want to be when they grow up. On the next round, each one describes some aspect of what it will be like to be that—where you might live, what you might wear, what kind of shoes it takes, and so forth. The object is to keep remembering what you have been saying. When you leave out any one of the things on your list, you are out of the game.

"When I grow up, I'm gonna be a cowboy," I said, leading off one day. I like to start, hoping that one day what will come out of my mouth is what I might actually be when I grow up.

My daughter quickly said, "When I grow up, I'm gonna be a cheerleader."

From the backseat, my son sang out, "When I grow up, I'm gonna be a fireman." He loves this game. He has a great affinity for the uniforms that go with various occupations. If he is going to be a pirate, he dresses the part before he goes out to play. When he changes games, he changes clothes. The makers of Tide consider him to be at the very center of their marketing strategy.

Round and round we went. "When I grow up, I am gonna be a cowboy and have a white horse and I will have a black hat and I am gonna live on a big ranch in Montana," I said.

"When I grow up, I'm gonna be a cheerleader and wear white cheerleading shoes and cheer for Vander-

bilt and do flips whenever we score a basket," said my
daughter.

My son was in the middle of his fireman with a
red hat and polka-dotted dog and ladder truck
round. But four rounds is about the maximum for
him, and from the backseat there was a tentative beginning. "When I grow up, I'm gonna be . . . uh,
uh . . ." and then a long and painful pause.

During the pause my daughter got excited because she knew that one of her competitors was
about to go down in defeat. My son began to get a
look of resignation on his face as he foresaw his im-
pending elimination from the contest. And I started
into the hint routine I often performed in the rearview mirror, hoping my son would see me mouthing
the word *fireman*. But he was not looking at me; his
eyes were closed in concentration as a few minutes
went by slowly.

Suddenly his face brightened, and with a big grin,
the grin of the suddenly all-knowing, Geoffrey an-
nounced, "When I grow up I am going to be *Geoffrey!*"
We declared him world champion for life right on
the spot.

When I was thirteen, I knew exactly what I wanted to be when I grew up. It was the most wonderful and fulfilling and exciting and magical thing I could think of. I somehow had the sense that it was what I was made for, could be good at, and loved to do. I could close my eyes and see myself doing it, right down to the hat and shoes of it.

Furthermore, I was very confident that it was what God thought I ought to do as well. Though I could not articulate it in such terms then, I realize now that I had the sense that I had been gifted for it, given the personality that goes with it, and blessed with an environment in which to grow into it. It was the sort of thing that seemed to just flow out of me, came easy to me, and I looked forward to spending a lifetime doing it.

And lo and behold, twenty-five years later I quit what I was doing to become it. At the time I finally made the choice, people asked me how I could do that—leave everything and do something so risky and so unlucrative and so abnormal. Yet the real risk was to not do it, to continue doing something with my life that did not have much to do with who I really was.

"How we spend our days is, of course, how we spend our lives," writes Annie Dillard. "What we do with this hour, and that one, is what we are doing." I finally realized that I was no longer willing to spend any more hours not being who I was—for love or money or anything else.

"In the beginning was the Word, and that Word came and dwelt among us," wrote John. And later, God only knows how much later, another word was whispered into the darkness—and here I am among us too. Different word, of course; same Voice, though.

The Hebrew word for it is *dabhar,* "God spoke." It is the word found in Genesis to describe the way the world came to be. God spoke the light. God spoke the Christ. God spoke Robert. God spoke Fred and Annie and Sara and Cindy and Alan and Barbara— and you, too, whatever your name is.

Seminary professor Robert Mulholland writes that we are "an incarnate word, spoken by God, still being spoken by God, a word of grace, of reconciliation, truth, love, healing. But," he goes on, "our word is often garbled. Part of our struggle here is to liberate the word within us so that it can be spoken clearly."

———❧———

Frederick Buechner has written that we spend our lives in search. We search, he says, "for a self to be, for other selves to love, and for work to do." And I believe that it is possible for the fruit of that search for work to do to be aligned with what God dreamed we would be when we were whispered into being. But how to do it, how to ungarble that word so that it can be heard clearly within ourselves, is the hard part.

"There is no shortage of good days," declares Dillard. "It is good lives that are hard to come by."

———❧———

In searching for a self to be, we can get bogged down in our own sense of uncertainty about who we really are. Sometimes we are so mystified by and about our own selves that we run from them, and put off the search to some other time when we will not have a career to manage or money to make or promises to keep.

And gradually we come to see that finding other selves to love seems easier somehow if we do not try to include a lot of folks who happen to be too different from what others think are the proper sort of other selves for us to love.

In our society, it is more highly valued to concentrate our energies on finding work to do. Which may be why so many of us have the idea that what we do is who we are. And why so many of us do something with the hope that if we do it long enough and well enough and successfully enough, we will become somebody.

In an age when the first question a stranger will ask us on meeting us for the first time is *What do you do?,* when society seems to be saying to us that what we accomplish is what really counts, when a list of achievements is taken to be the true measure of a person, it can be difficult to remember that first and foremost we are called to be Geoffrey. Or Angela or Sherry or Arthur or Frances, or whatever your name is.

—❧—

Over the course of the twenty-five years between the time when I knew who I was to be and the time when I actually began to be it every day, virtually every decision I made that had anything to do with my education, my relationships, or my career was made for the wrong reasons. They were reasons that had to do with what I thought other folks would have me do, with what was acceptable to those who seemed to be in charge. Some of those choices turned out okay, and some of them led to pretty miserable failures.

In our age of individualism and self-reliance, it is not very fashionable to say that one has regrets about the past. But it is dishonest of us to say that we do not. If the choice were to be made now between the hell that I lived in for various times in my life— anger, divorce, loneliness, depression, fear of fail- ure—then I am as glad as anyone to be where I am today. And I am perfectly capable of swimming in the existential stream that says that all of those things were necessary in order for me to be where I am today, a place in which I am very happy. But I do

not for one moment imagine that all of the things
that have happened to me, and all of the terrible
things I have done to others, were imagined for me
by the One who dreamed me up.

When we are young and are wrestling with choices
about the future, we are very often asked, and ask
ourselves: "What are you going to do when you grow
up?" It is the wrong question. What we are going to *do*
is not who we *are*.

When it was time for me to make choices, I should
have been wrestling with another question. I should
have been asking, "Who am I going to be when I
grow up?" What I then went on to do with that
should have been a reflection of who I was to be, a reflection of the word that was whispered into me. I
should have been looking for work to do that would
sustain and nurture who I am (who I *be,* if you will). I
was then, and am still, the only person on earth who
has any clue at all as to what was whispered into me
in the depths of my mother's womb. Everyone else is
just guessing, and their guesses are a lot less well in-
formed than mine. God whispered the word *Robert*
into *me,* no one else. If I can not hear that word, no

one can. If I do not hear that word, no one will. If I do hear it and fail to act upon it, no one will be the word called *Robert* that God spoke.

Rabbi Zusya, one of the great wisdom teachers of the Hebrew tradition, once said, "In the world to come I shall not be asked: 'Why were you not Moses?' I shall be asked: 'Why were you not Zusya?'"

The will of the One who sent us is that we be the one who was sent. What we do is meant to be lived out of the context of discovering and becoming the person we are.

———

If enough of us were to ungarble our words, perhaps God's story might be more clearly heard and understood. Perhaps the song that God sings into the wind that whispers all around us in the trees would be on more lips and taught to more children. My friend Russell Montfort once remarked that he suspects that "we die with half our music left in us." Maybe we do not know the words to our own song.

And it is not just our own little melody that suffers; the whole chorus is not as good. If you leave out enough of the words, even the Song of the whole universe will sound funny.

The Song needs my word. It is not the same song without it. And I am the only one who has ever heard it, the only one who can ever listen to its echo deep inside and know whether or not the life that I am living—what I am doing with my hours and days and work and other selves to love—rhymes with it, and sings it clearly at all.

Six

Deliver us from the service of self alone
that we may do the work you have given us to do,
in truth and beauty and for the common good.
For the sake of the One who came among us
as one who serves.

A Collect for Vocation in Daily Work
The Book of Common Prayer

I SPENT AN AFTERNOON
once wandering and wondering in the plaza of a
great cathedral in Germany. There was a lot to wonder about there—the sheer beauty of the place, the
crowds of people who had come from all over the
world to see such a thing, the architecture, and the
workmanship itself. But what I found myself wondering about mostly that day, and still do, is the people who built it. And the people who dreamed it.

My working knowledge of the actual process of
cathedral building is pretty limited. However, it does
seem reasonable to assume that if it took a couple of
hundred years or so to build one, then the people
who dreamed it up never actually saw it completed.
In fact, whole generations would have passed between the time the dream was dreamed and the time

the choir made its first grand processional through the nave to the great high altar that the dreamers had envisioned.

Somewhere there must be stories of families who worked on a cathedral for generations. I suspect there are stories of neighbors and schoolmates, whole villages even, who spent their entire lives as stonemasons and woodworkers and ditchdiggers and carpenters for the cathedral. Stories of people who cut the glass that went into the windows that a neighbor's cousin had cut the stones for back before their grandfather was born.

A cathedral is a testimony to a lot of the best things about us: creativity, hard work, devotion, patience, craftsmanship, ingenuity. But it is also a testimony to dreams and those who believe in them. Someone dreams of a great house of worship, and someone else dreams of where it might be built. Someone dreams of where to find the stone for it, and then somebody dreams up a scheme to acquire the land rights. Then a whole lot of somebodies get caught up in the tide of the great dream and start cutting stones and hauling logs, raising money and driving nails, negotiating contracts and pounding iron. Whatever else such people are, they are dreamers.

If you had asked any one of those who built the cathedral at Cologne what they were, the answers would most likely not have been very poetic: "I am a carpenter"; "I am a blacksmith"; "I am only a seamstress"; "Just a stonecutter."

If you ask God, you would hear something very different, I expect. For without them, there is no cathedral.

———∞∞∞———

In *Blue Highways,* his fascinating story of his pilgrimage across America, William Least Heat Moon tells of meeting a man who takes him to task for the way he uses the words *job* and *work* interchangeably. "Oughten do that," the man says. "A job is what you force yourself to pay attention to for money. With work you don't have to force yourself. There are a lot of jobs in this country, and that's good because they keep people occupied. That's why they call them 'occupations.'"

We spend our days doing what we do for all kinds of reasons. It is the work we have been given to do or what we have found to do. Some of us do work that seems to have found us in some way, for better or worse. A fair number of us do things that we love to do, whatever that might mean to us, but if you ask very many people if that is so for them, not as many of them will say yes as you might have thought or hoped.

How do we come to choose what it is that we spend our days doing? Would we choose it again if we could? Did we choose it today, or has it simply carried us along somehow?

I once worked for a very long time in a place where I did not really feel very good at all about the things that we made and sold. In another place I worked among some people who lived their lives and saw the world in such different ways than I did that I could hardly bear to be around them. But I kept going back, day after day, not really sure why, knowing only that the financial realities that seemed to govern my life at the time demanded that I hold on somehow. I could not run the risk of not finding anything better, so I sold my life by the hour to someone who had no idea of the purchase they were making. But then I had no idea of what I was selling either.

It is terrifyingly easy to find oneself doing one's work without any real sense of the meaning of it. I have spent a lot of time involved in a workshop that helps people come to see the spiritual gifts that are at work in them and in their lives. One young woman that I remember—a young woman whose shyness was painful to see, whose sense of her own self was so low that she could hardly look you in the eye—told a group of us that she was sure God had not given her any gifts that could be used for ministry to others. "I am just a night nurse in a children's hospital," she said, almost embarrassed. What would it have taken I wondered—a clerical collar or a seat on the board, a medical degree or a bigger salary, a house on a hill or a big shiny car—to help her see that she was gifted in a way that is more ministry in an evening than many of us do in a lifetime?

"Just a carpenter." "Just a night nurse." *Just nobody,* I think to myself.

I wonder how many of us—teachers, doctors, parents, farmers, nurses, day-care workers, waiters—do the work of the Christ in this world and do not know it. Why is it that we in the church have so often failed to see, and share with each other, the ways in which one can see the gifts of healing, knowledge, hospitality, mercy, service, and the rest at work in our lives and in the lives of those around us?

In our society, we far too often measure our work by the standards of the American Dream, a phrase stuck on us by a person who evidently believed that Calvin Coolidge was right when he said, "The chief business of the American people is business."

I confess to you that my ideas about the American Dream are something less than mainstream these days. My car is almost ten years old, my shoes are worn, my television is not hooked to a cable or a satellite dish, my driveway is not big enough for a boat (though it does have enough room for the basketball goal my best friend bought me for my forty-first birthday). My three friends will tell you, however, that they have never seen me happier.

It may well be that the business of America is business, but the business of the Dreamer has always been and always will be something else altogether. And the business of selling our lives by the hour, doing work that we do not want to do or being people that we do not want to be—in the name of piling up treasures that have more to do with what we want or think we ought have than with what we need, treasures that have more to do with what shines rather than what sustains—is hardly what the Dreamer envisioned.

———

We do not talk much about building cathedrals these days. But we should, I think.

Saint Paul once wrote to his friends in Ephesus that there is "a spiritual dwelling for God" being built among us and that we all are a part of it. A great temple, Saint Paul called it—a cathedral, I call it—that was dreamed by the Dreamer and is meant for us to build.

Its foundation was laid by the prophets and the apostles, by the early church and the desert fathers and mothers, by the saints who are revered and the saints whose names are unknown to us. The cathedral that is being built here includes all of them and all of us, all who have gone before and all who will come after. We, and all that we are—dreams, hopes, gifts, hours, days, work, sweat—are meant to be stones in the cathedral of the Dreamer.

In many ways, it does not matter whether we are preachers or poets, stonecutters or schoolteachers, accountants or architects. Nor does it particularly matter if we are woodworkers or water carriers, missionaries or metalworkers. What matters is that we dream our dreams and hope our hopes and do our work as though we believe in the Dreamer and the dream for the cathedral that is being built here. For without us, it will not be built.

"You can't eat for eight hours a day nor drink for eight hours a day nor make love for eight hours a day," wrote William Faulkner. "All you can do for eight hours a day is work."

We may as well get used to the idea. And do our work with as much joy and abandon as we can muster. Not because it will make us rich or powerful or any of the other measures that have been given to us by those who would replace the dream of the

Dreamer with something less, something that can be tacked onto a political platform and hammered into marketing whizzes in graduate schools. But because it part of the cathedral being built here.

———❦———

My best friend, who happens to be married to me, and I were in New York City once and decided to visit the Cathedral of Saint John the Divine. My friends back home would have been very nervous had they known how close we came to never getting on the plane and flying home that day.

For one thing, we nearly got lost in the place. When it is completed, it will be the largest cathedral in the world, large enough for the Statue of Liberty to fit inside its dome. It occupies thirteen acres of gardens and grounds. It has seven chapels, three choirs, and a dozen bays surrounding the nave, each bay roughly the size of the little church where two hundred people watched my wife and me get married.

In the space of three hours on the morning we were there, there were several hundred tourists, two funerals, a wedding, a baptism, an orchestral rehearsal, a high school graduation exercise, an organ rehearsal, and a big sale in the book and gift shop. The stonecutters in the adjacent stone yard had the day off, but the gardeners were out in full force, as were those who had come to light candles and say prayers, and those of us who had made it just in time for morning prayers in one of the smaller chapels. All of which seemed to me like a pretty busy Saturday schedule for a place that has been under construction since 1877 and is still a long way from being finished. If the cathedral was not yet ready for people to worship and serve and pray and celebrate and mourn and offer oblations in, no one could tell as far as I could see.

Our intention had been to run uptown and look through the cathedral, taxi back downtown to wander through an art gallery, and still have plenty of time to catch our late-afternoon flight. As we stood in the back of the nave, however, it took about the same amount of time for our eyes to adjust to the darkness as it did for us to realize that we were standing in the presence of as much art as we had ever seen and maybe were ever going to need.

A lot of things make me weep. I come from a long and distinguished line of folks whose eyes will tear up at anything that is even slightly moving. These days I am particularly moved by places large and small where, as I read in the San Fernando Cathedral in San Antonio, the "floors have been worn down by the thousands of feet moving in pilgrimage." We had not been standing there very long when I felt a lump start to rise in my throat.

I turned to look at my wife as she looked through the nave to the great high altar some two hundred yards away. In the mysterious light that filtered in from the stained-glass windows high above us, light punctuated by the flickering of hundreds of candles left by the morning's penitents and petitioners and pilgrims, I saw that her eyes were glistening as well.

"Oh, my," she whispered, without ever turning her eyes toward me. "That someone would do something like this for the glory of God."

Later, over lunch, comparing notes about what we wanted to do as soon as we got back across the street to the cathedral, we fell to making plans to volunteer. I was going to be a stonecutter, and she was going to throw herself at the feet of the rose gardeners, holding up her green thumb and reciting the Latin names for roses until they gave her a job. Fortunately, at least for the sake of those at home who were counting on us to be on that plane in the afternoon, we never did run into anything that looked like a personnel office, and we dashed for the airport and made our flight just in time.

If I am to do anything "like this for the glory of God," it will have to be at my house, in my work, with my dreams. And if it is not completed, I will be in good company. The biggest cathedral I have ever seen is still under construction. The Cathedral of the Dreamer is still being imagined into being.

———— ✎ ————

On the wall of one of the cathedral bays at Saint John's, the one called the Poet's Corner, there is an inscription carved into the stone that quotes Willa Cather: "Thy will be done in art as it is in heaven." Amen, I say. And in plumbing and paper pushing and publishing as well. And in teachering and board-membering and doctoring and bricklaying, for that matter. Or in whatever else it turns out is the work that you and I are given to do by the One who is looking forward to seeing our "stone" in the long-awaited Cathedral. The work that we do for the Cathedral is in front of us each day. It is in the work that we do for each other, with each other, and beside each other. It is work that we can and must do "for the sake of the One who came among us as one who serves."

Not because we will see the Cathedral in our lifetime or even see our own work completed or because we will be hailed as the cornerstone itself, but because it is part and parcel of the reason the Dreamer sent us here.

Seven

———⊷⊶———

Grant us such an awareness of your mercies we pray,
that with truly thankful hearts
we may give you praise,
not only with our lips but in our lives,
by giving up ourselves to your service
and walking before you in holiness and righteousness
all our days.

From The Prayers of the People
The Book of Common Prayer

I CONSIDER MYSELF ONE of those who is woefully ill-equipped for life in the twentieth century. The twenty-first century is something that I do not even want to contemplate.

The speed and pace of our life here in this country, the noise and the demand of it, the sheer unadulterated motion of it, are almost too much for me to cope with. We live in a time when the admonition to stop and smell the roses can be a hit song or an advertising slogan but the reality is that we are more likely to buy antique-rose air freshener on a string and hook it around our rearview mirror and keep our cars window rolled up.

I was in a restaurant once where an old colleague of mine came in for lunch with his new wife. Having not seen him in a while, I stopped on my way out to say hello. About two sentences into the conversation, his pocket rang and he pulled a telephone from it. While he answered the call, his wife began to explain to me that they had come in for their anniversary lunch date. Then there was another ring, and she pulled a telephone from her purse and left me standing there to greet the waiter. I ordered champagne for them and headed for the door. I hope they had the presence of mind to put their telephones in the ice bucket while they toasted their life together.

I was in the music business with this same man for almost ten years. I know exactly what his job is and how it works. Enough to know that in a week, maybe even an hour, no one would remember the conversation he just had on the phone. I, however, have never forgotten that one of his old friends and his new wife were less important than the phone call. If his third wife is still around, she may not have forgotten, either.

———❧———

Why do we live the way that we live? What is all of our noise and frantic racing around about?

Why do we book our schedules so tightly that we can hardly breathe and then complain that we are too worn out to enjoy ourselves? "Time may be money," sings James Taylor, "but your money won't buy time."

Why do we look for a boy to cut our grass, a landscaper to mulch our flower beds, a golf cart to carry our clubs, a sack boy to carry our groceries, and then get up at the crack of dawn to get shin splints from running on pavement in the name of exercise?

Why is it that we turn on the television the minute we wake up, put telephones in our cars and boats and pockets, plan something to do for every night of the week, and then wish we had time for a little peace and quiet?

Why do we visit a sanctuary one hour a week (two hours if the sermon gets out of hand or the stewardship chairman is making a pitch), watch a carefully choreographed service of worship (or a carefully spontaneous one, for that matter), and then frequently complain that we cannot hear God speaking to us at all?

Having once observed that the majority of us lead "lives of quiet desperation," Thoreau, of course, would not be surprised to hear that the mass of men and women still lead lives of desperation. But our desperation is more noisy now, it seems to me, the technological age having had its way even with our anxiety.

———∞∞∞———

When I was thirty-eight years old, I finally stopped believing in Santa Claus. It happened exactly 365 days after the Christmas Eve when I made a solemn vow to myself never to spend another Night of the Child wrestling tricycle parts and wrenches at midnight on the floor of my living room.

Prior to that I had marked Christmas Eve with the time-honored ritual of those who had gone before me, following the basic pattern of the day that had been taught to me. In the late afternoon, after a day spent frantically buying and wrapping presents and packages, one dressed up in one's Sunday clothes and headed off to the ranking grandparent's house for dinner. One ate one's dinner in the crush of too many people and not enough chairs, all conversation drowned out by children asking if the adults were ever going to stop stuffing themselves and open presents. After dinner, after some of the crowd had cleaned up the dishes, one opened presents, thereby knocking off about three months' pay in about ten minutes, oohed and ahhed a bit over the haul one had made, picked up all the paper, packed up one's car, hauled one's kids home and wrestled them into bed, and then started bringing this year's Santa Claus offerings out of their various and sundry hiding places.

Invariably, about midnight, one was generally staring into the poorly written assembly instructions of the one thing that needed to be put together that would take the most time, and require the most muttering under one's breath. And that, if not ready and under the tree, would be the one thing that broke the back of Santa's big day. The search for batteries, of course, was still to come. One of the least celebrated bits of the wisdom of the wise men is that they chose gifts marked No Assembly Required.

About three in the morning on the Christmas Eve in question, it occurred to me that something astonishing had taken place in Bethlehem that night and that I had missed it, again. Somewhere there were shepherds abandoning their flocks and running across darkened meadows in wonder and joy, singing songs with the heavenly host, while I was here nicking my fingers on wing nuts that did not fit and trying to not wake up the children so that Santa Claus could get the credit for the things I had bought.

So the next Christmas Eve, I found my way to a big stone house of worship that was open at midnight for a crowd of people who were hushed and breathless with anticipation. The bells rang softly, candles were lit, the scent of pine wreaths filled the air. White-robed singers, followed by black-robed ministers looking for all the world like wise men and women from somewhere east of here, made their stately way through the nave singing a song that began to tell the story of that night so long ago. Faces all around me were lit with candlelight and hope; the room fairly glowed. Songs and stories, prayers and promises, homilies and hopes were offered up. Then came the invitation to the Table set before us, set by Immanuel himself. Slowly, singing carols softly to ourselves and to each other, we stood in the aisle and waited our turn to kneel and take the bread and the wine, to be given the gifts by the wise men and women who served us on His behalf.

When everyone had been served and the last soft
carol sung, there was stillness for a long moment.
The choir stood in its place. One of the ministers
raised his arms and motioned for us to stand as well.
As we watched in silence and wonder, the ministers
moved reverently from place to place in the chancel,
removing the deep purple vestments of Advent, re-
placing them with the bright, golden-white vestments signifying the coming of the Light into this
room, this night, this world.

The lights seemed to grow brighter, the faces to
shine even more as tears glistened and began to wander their way down our cheeks to the corners of awe-
struck smiles of unspeakable joy.

The great organ rumbled into the first notes of
the recessional hymn. The ministers and the choir
and then we who sat in the pews began to sing the
song of the angels: "Joy to the world, the Lord has
come." Row by row, we took up our places in the procession that moved down the aisles, singing with all
our hearts. Wendy Wright has called this "the season
in which we rise up on tiptoes to dance," and on that
night we rose up and we danced down the aisle to
the joyous song, past our friends and fellow pilgrims,

in procession with the shepherds and angels and wise men and the innkeeper who had come to see what was going on in his stable that was causing such a fuss. We sang and smiled and danced in procession with all those who had annually awaited and faithfully anticipated the birth of the Child and the coming of the Light.

We sang and danced our way out into the crisp night air. Incredibly, snow was falling—a strange occurrence for our town at that time of year. As we drove home, the song would not stop: "Let every heart prepare him room, let every heart prepare him room, let every heart prepare him room." I sang the song to my children, already asleep, as I laid them in their beds. I sang it to myself, hoping against hope that it would indeed take root in me and in my heart and in my house. I sang it to the Silence of the blue-black sky, gratefully acknowledging the One who had said again, "Let there be light," and who had given us a name by which to call it.

One of the lessons of the saints that it seems the Protestants failed to pack with them when they headed west in their little boats toward the New World is that there are rhythms to this madness we call our lives and that those rhythms can be learned and lived. Rhythms that mirror the story of God's relationship with creation and humanity, rhythms that hold us together as a people. Rhythms that we can use to hold up the stories of our own lives into the Light of each day, each week, each season. They are rhythms whose names we do not by and large recognize any longer, whose meanings we do not understand, whose symbols we no longer hold dear, whose prayers we do not pray, whose fruits we no longer taste.

The rhythm of the Mass itself—Praise, Confession, the Word, Sending Forth—can be a way for us to see where we are as decisions and changes and challenges come to us.

The liturgical calendar—Advent, Christmas, Epiphany, Lent, Easter, Pentecost, Kingdomtide—can teach us to wait patiently in our darkness for the coming of the Light, to believe once again that God has come among us, to seek the One Among Us in everything and everyone we see, to walk the long and bittersweet road to Jerusalem, to live the life of the resurrection in the shadow of the cross, to receive and unleash the Spirit anew in our world, to take up our journey again and again from slavery to freedom to the wilderness to the promised land.

The Eucharist itself, with its steady and startling reminder that the Body of Christ is meant to be taken, blessed, broken, and shared again and again and again, can teach us to see our lives as food for the journey for others, as sustenance for each other for the building of the Kingdom itself.

But the calendar of the church, the ancient rhythms of the life of the faithful, teaches us none of these things if we do not live in them.

If we observe Advent at the mall, spend the night of the Nativity building tricycles, kick off Lent with a ski trip, spend Easter at the beach, we are not likely to come face-to-face with the One Who Comes.

If we take the Eucharist once a year, take no time to be apart and to listen for the Voice, give God some directives and pointers for five minutes a day and call it prayer, and do none of the things that the faithful who traveled this road before us would remind us to do, then we are likely to only talk to God and never hear a response.

A life lived in the hope and anticipation of hearing the Voice that whispered us into being and seeks to speak to us about what we are here to learn and be and do—a prayerful life, if you will—is, as Henri Nouwen writes, "a life in which nothing, absolutely nothing, is done, said, or understood independently of the One who is the origin and purpose of our existence."

We do not have to seek these rhythms, these ways of listening, and appropriate them for our very own. It is not a question of salvation. It is, however, a question of living the life we were dreamed into being to live. "You do not have to sit alone in the dark," notes Annie Dillard. "If, however, you want to look at the stars, you will find that darkness is necessary."

We are under no obligation to live the seasons of the story or do anything else to bring ourselves to attention if we do not want to. "You do not have to do these things," Dillard suggests, "unless you want to know God. They work on you, not him."

But if we would know God, and if we would come to know something of what God wanted us to know so badly that he was willing to part with us for a time while we came here to learn what we can learn only by being here, then we will have to pay attention. To do so, we may well need to learn and practice the rhythms of the ancient dance of the Ancient of Days.

To cut ourselves off from this world of the ancient dance is to cut ourselves off from the community of saints. It is to live our lives as though we, in our own private wisdom, will find a way to a life of devotion and sanctity without the aid of those who traveled the road before. Such a posture is foolishness. It amounts to looking for the stars at noon.

And Thoreau would tell us, it leads to a life of desperation, whether that life be quiet or noisy or otherwise.

Eight

---∞∞∞---

Deliver us when we draw near to you
from coldness of heart and wanderings of mind,
so that with steadfast thoughts and kindled affections
we may worship you in spirit and in truth.

A Prayer Before Worship
The Book of Common Prayer

I MET A MAN WHO ONCE spent a year alone in a cave in the Middle East. He was not very impressive to look at—graying, close-cropped hair, three inches shorter than me in height, plaid short-sleeved shirt and old khakis, some sort of lace-up earth shoes on his feet. He had no rings on his fingers, no Rolex watch, no stuff to add to his presence in any way. He had a quiet voice, well-worn face and hands. Until I met him the only eyes that had ever held me in such a way belonged to my father. I had no idea that one could look at a stranger in that way.

I learned that his religious order had sent him to the cave in order to pray. He took with him two books, a crucifix, and some candles. On a specific day each week, someone from his community would deliver food and water and a change of clothes to a prearranged spot at the foot of the mountain. The next day he would go down to pick up his things and leave his other clothes to be washed and brought back again. He did not see or speak to another human being that year. He spoke to and listened for only God.

Seven times a day he would recite the prayers from the tradition of his community. Seven times a day he would repeat the words that had been prayed for hundreds of years by those who would hear the Voice. And then he would listen.

The recitation of the prayers, he said, was not to get God's attention; the prayers were merely the offering he made. They were prayed to bring him to attention.

Fifteen years later, the love that had been born there in the silence and darkness of that cave in the heart of a man who was willing to come to attention was given to me without words, across a book table set up in the hallway of a crowded convention center. The look in his eyes changed the way I have come to look at others that I meet. The story I heard him tell of his journey changed the way I have come to see my own story. The prayers that he said in the cave all those years before we met changed my life.

———— ⊗⊗⊗ ————

One morning, very early, sitting in a chair in the studio in my house, trying to begin to write whatever it was that was on my plate to write that day, watching the sun come up in a clear summer sky, I began to wonder just what might happen to me if I made a conscious choice to learn how to pray.

I was raised around people who prayed. They prayed through, prayed over, prayed on request, prayed before dinner, prayed with their children at bedtime. And I grew up in a part of the country where they still say prayers before football games; they are not about to let the law of the land interfere with their traditions. I had no baggage at all about whether or not God was listening or would answer or anything. I just had a deep and growing sense that with all of the prayers I had heard or even said in my life, I knew very little about living a life of prayer or about what my life would become in the process of trying to discover and live such a life.

So I decided to make the "journey toward prayer," as some call it, just as soon as I could get some sense of the direction in which to head.

———— ⚬⚬⚬ ————

A man came to give a series of classes in the church I was attending. He came shuffling into the first session, in khakis and a tweed jacket, looking for all the world like a professor who had spent the vast majority of his life digging around in obscure books written by obscure people. It turned out that this was exactly the case.

He threw around words and terms that I had never heard before: *spiritual formation* and *spirituality, prayer of the heart* and *centering* and *contemplation.* He quoted saints and mystics and hermits and anchorites and the desert fathers and mothers. He talked about daily offices and silence and praying the Psalms.

And he was quiet and shy and funny and absolutely unflappable. After a few classes, I asked him to have lunch with me. I was hopeful that he could give me some clues as to where I should begin my journey.

His advice was not exactly what this good Naz-
arene turned Methodist expected to hear from a
Southern Baptist university professor right here on
the buckle of the Bible Belt.

"Follow the Catholics," he said. "They are the
only ones who know."

My knowledge of the Catholic tradition was lim-
ited to say the least. *Industrial-strength limited* is probably
a good term to describe it. But Ben showed me some
places to begin to read, and I began.

If one begins a journey toward prayer, tracing the
path of the ones who have walked the way of prayer
faithfully for centuries, one cannot go very far without running into Catholic monks and nuns. They
will lead you back to people like Saint Francis, Saint
Benedict, and Julian of Norwich—those who spent
their lives keeping the prayer of church alive. They
will lead you to the desert, to the stories of the abbas
and ammas, to the hermits and anchorites who went
to the wilderness to pray. And those stories lead
you to the early church, to the Jewish believers who

shaped the life of Christian prayer from the traditions and patterns of the Hebrew faith, the faith handed down to them by the ancients.

To whatever small degree I had ever considered it, I had always thought of the desert fathers and mothers as people who had gone into the desert to pray in order to avoid the secular society that was being pressed in on them by the "pagans" who were in power politically. I saw them as the very devout, and the very eccentric, men and women who had finally taken all they could and had headed off to a cave to pray, muttering under their breath at those pagans as they went.

Their stories tell a different story: if they were muttering under their breath as they headed out into the wilderness, it was the Christians they were upset with, not the pagans. They were not particularly angry with the so-called secular society; they were upset with the church folks.

In the first two or three centuries after Christ, Christians had been persecuted and harassed almost constantly, which gave rise to a deep need to maintain a common life of prayer as a way to stay strong in the face of the dangers they faced. They were primarily Jewish believers, and the ones who were Gentiles were taught the faith by Jewish believers. The life of prayer they lived in those early days mirrored what had always been the life of the people who had listened for and followed the God of Moses.

They rose in the night to chant the psalms; during the day they said the prescribed prayers at the traditional hours of nine, noon, and three. They shared a common meal in the evening, accompanied by liturgies and prayers from the Hebrew tradition. The meal was followed by the Eucharist and prayers of thanksgiving. They observed Wednesdays and Fridays as days of penance and fasting.

The third century brought good news and bad. The good news was that the Emperor Constantine got religion, as the old folks would say. The bad news was that he declared it the state religion. The persecutions were over, the institution was born, and gradually the practice of the life of prayer began to fade away.

So those who still sought to live such a life headed to the desert to pray, to live the life of the faithful that had been handed down to them by those who had gone before. They went to the desert because no one else wanted to. And they went to the desert because Jesus, the one they wanted to follow, had gone there before them as well.

⸰⸗⸏⸘

When the disciples asked Jesus to teach them to pray, he responded with a prayer that was largely constructed from phrases taken from Jewish liturgical prayers. The words he groaned from the cross as he died—"Into your hands I commit my spirit"—were quoted from the end of the traditional prayers that had been said at sundown by the faithful for centuries before him.

Many of the parables and stories he told had roots in the Jewish wisdom literature that was contemporary to his times; others had told some of those stories before him as we tell them after him even now. It is less likely that he quoted from the scriptures and the psalms because he dictated them, as some would have us believe, than it is that he did so because he studied and prayed them in the way the faithful had taught him to do, until they had become a part of the very fabric of his thought and life.

His teaching and healing and encountering people in the synagogues was no accident. Where else would you expect to find him and the people to whom he was to proclaim the coming of the Kingdom but at the houses of prayer where those who sought God gathered for prayer and worship day in and day out?

"We are the Body of Christ," we say in our creeds and sing in our songs and print in our books. It is good to remind ourselves of this because it is true. And it is right for us to see ourselves as the hands and feet of Christ in this world and to see ourselves as responsible for announcing the good news, proclaiming the Kingdom, telling the Story. But it has been a long time since many of us have thought much about praying as he prayed, about praying the prayer of Christ. Most of us were taught that he had only the one, the one that begins with the word *Abba*.

Perhaps we who would follow him, we who seek to be his Body in this world, would do well to pray as he prayed, to pray as his first followers prayed, to seek to live a life of prayer and devotion as did those who first followed him.

———— ∞ ————

I have a friend who prays a kind of modified version of the monastic offices each day. He does not talk about it a lot—an example of Emilie Griffin's observation that "people who pray, really pray, do not talk about it much." But I talk with him about it some; he is an old friend of mine.

He is not a Catholic; he is not a monk. He is not ordained. He is not even college educated. He has acquired his habits of prayer by wandering around in books and churches, picking up bits and pieces there, mostly wondering and trying and hoping. The prayer book he uses is largely a construction of his own making, woven together from threads and bits from several Christian traditions.

I have known him a long time, and as much as I like him, I have to tell you he most certainly is not holy. I have seen him do some good for other folks, but I have also seen him being just as angry and selfish and lazy as the best and worst of us. I have seen him stumble and fall, make bad choices, and look like a fool. No one else on earth that I know of can make me angrier, faster. Or laugh as hard, now that I think of it.

I think of him sometimes on his knees in his front room in the little house where he lives in a rather ordinary neighborhood. I can hear him as he repeats the thanksgivings and the psalms, I can see him reading the scriptures, and I can imagine the line of his jaw as he sits in the silence, listening, listening. I can hear him whisper the Our Father and the Gloria and the canticle of the day.

I can hear him as he simply names the names of everyone he knows and everyone who has come to mind since the last time he prayed. He makes no requests, specifies no ailments or conditions or hopes or petitions. He simply says the name and says the Kyrie, and then he listens. He says that sometimes he hears that there is a way he can be Christ to someone this day and that sometimes he can even muster up the courage to do it. Sometimes he hears nothing at all. He also says that when he says their names, he is with them, wherever they may be that day.

I asked him once why he prays this way. "This is the way they used to pray, a long time ago. So someone has to, I think." After another moment he said, "So I do."

—⊗∞⊗—

These ancient traditions of the life of the devout—praying the psalms, saying the offices, meditating on the scriptures, contemplating the mysteries of God, living a life that is in and yet not of the society around us—were once thought of highly enough by those who would hear the Voice that they taught them to those who lived in the Middle East two thousand years ago. They were at the center of the life of the early church itself. They were kept alive by the desert fathers and mothers, and sustained over the centuries by monks and nuns in the Roman and the Orthodox communions.

But somehow they got lost along the way. Perhaps the circuit riders could not find room for them in the saddlebags. Whatever happened, they did not make it to many of us who grew up in Protestant churches in America in the twentieth century. My friend told me to follow the Catholics because they brought with them the prayers of the faithful that are used "for the praise of God and for the sanctifying of each day . . . the very prayer which Christ Himself, together with his body, addresses to the Father," as the Catholic Church describes them.

When that prayer, and the life that it shapes and nurtures within us, was lost to us, we lost the deep and powerful practices and meanings of words like *contemplation, divine offices,* and *sacred reading.* We lost the discipline of praying the psalms, of practicing silence and retreat. We lost touch with the ways that the faithful had learned to bring themselves to attention. We lost our access to the world in which the Voice can speak to us. We lost the habits of the heart that can turn a life into a prayer that is prayed without ceasing.

⸘

Thomas Merton wrote that when he first arrived at the Abbey of Gethsemani, he came to believe that Gethsemani was the center of the universe, that it was the prayer of the monks living there that was keeping the world from flying apart at its increasingly well-worn seams. Not because these men were so holy, but simply because they prayed. He may or may not be right about their holding the world together, but there is no doubt about the fact that there is something powerful about being in the presence of those who are willing to come to attention.

Perhaps they were among the thirty-six.

In the Hebrew tradition, there is told the story of the thirty-six who are faithful—so faithful, in fact, that God refuses to have the world come to an end as long as they are alive. It is their devotion that holds the world together. No one but God knows who they are; even they themselves do not know.

I am not certain what you would find if you found them—lawyers, doctors, schoolteachers, homemakers, shortstops, maybe even the monks of Gethsemani. I do expect that you will find evidence that they live their lives in the rhythm of prayer that is prayed without ceasing, prayer that has been prayed until they themselves have become a prayer.

Nine

———⟨∞⟩———

You have made us one with your saints
in heaven and in earth.
Grant that in our pilgrimage,
we may always be supported by this fellowship
of love and prayer,
and know ourselves to be surrounded
by their witness to your power and mercy.

A Collect for the Communion of Saints
The Book of Common Prayer

THERE IS A PLACE I WENT
to every three months for two years to spend a week
in a community of prayer. There were about sixty of
us—by and large strangers to each other when we
began, brothers and sisters when our season together
had ended. I did not go there because I was holy; I
went there because I was hungry.

For a community built around a common desire
for prayer and silence, there was an extraordinary
amount of activity that went on each day. Most all
of it was wonderful stuff, and all of it done in the
name of worship and prayer, fellowship and community, or rest and reflection. Two teachers were invited
in each week to teach us about various and sundry
things concerning the spiritual life as they understood it. One of the regular parts of the instruction
was to send us all out for an hour of silence after each

lecture with a reflection assignment to do before we came back to the classroom for questions and answers and shared wonderings.

My friends in the community thought that I—as one who is regularly, and rightfully, accused of spending a good deal more time lost in reflection than perhaps I ought to be spending—must look forward to the reflection assignments. They just assumed that any sort of faculty-approved daydreaming would be right up my alley. The truth is that a call to "be reflective" is about as motivating to me as is a call to "be creative."

I hate to admit it, but I generally spent the reflecting hour seated on a bridge down by a creek that runs along the foot of the mountain behind the lodge, trying my best to look as though I was deep in thought, somewhere between contemplative and downright holy. I played a lot of Poohsticks to pass the time.

Poohsticks is a game where you drop sticks off one side of a bridge and watch them come out the other side. If the bridge is a wide one and you have some kids with you (these days, it gets harder and harder to find grown-ups who will play), the game

can get to be good fun as you dash back and forth
across the bridge to see whose sticks come out first.
(More extensive directions for the game, including
how to make up Hums—Songs You Make Up For
Any Occasion—and what to do if Eeyore comes out
from under the bridge with your stick, may be found
in *The House at Pooh Corner*, a book I often recommend
to people going on retreat.)

The particular bridge where I hid out during the
assigned reflection hour is a small one that was per-
fect for playing Poohsticks for One, or *poohstickus soli-
tarius*, as I named it one day after a lecture on *lectio
divina*. You could sit in the middle of the bridge and
look left as you threw the sticks in the creek and look
to the right to see them when they came out from
under the bridge. It was not as exciting as a full-blown
game with a bunch of first-graders, but it was sure
better than reflecting on demand. Poohsticks is not
a bad way to spend a portion of a week devoted to
prayer, but I kept pretty quiet about it. I was not sure
if some of the visiting gurus would buy it as a form of
meditatio.

"Draw a circle," said the instructor who was
teaching us about spiritual friendship one day, "and

then put in it those who have helped you on your journey toward God." The idea of drawing circles on paper did not strike me as particularly appealing, but it did occur to me that this particular reflection assignment might be something that one could do down by the creek with very tiny Poohsticks. So for once I went off to reflect about what I was supposed to when I was supposed to. Along the way down the path to the creek, I decided to call the new game Saintsticks.

<hr />

I am a fourth-generation churchgoer. Maybe even fifth- or sixth-generation, though the written family history has no record of whether or not our ancestor who came down the river into my home state of Tennessee actually ever joined the church after he boarded the flatboat that was heading west from North Carolina. I have heard whispers about his being released from jail, but none about his being elected to the Church board.

I do know, however, that one of my great-grandfathers was a charter member of a denomination; one of my grandfathers was a publisher of religious music

Monday through Friday and old-time, arm-waving, necktie-loosening, hymnbook-thumping song leader on Sundays; another has been a church organist all his life; and my father was a minister and a church-music publisher and a writer and a retreat leader.

As one of the fourth generation of Bensons to attend the particular church where I grew up, built on the very spot where my great-grandfather was named the first treasurer of the denomination, a considerable portion of the folks in the church knew me and prayed for me and taught Sunday school at me and took me on youth retreats and other things. It was a place full of the sort of people who come to mind when one sets out to play Saintsticks.

So I headed to a place beyond the Poohsticks bridge where I knew no one else would be. It was a little stretch of beach along the creek that has no big boulders to sit on, the sort of place where one can never quite get comfortable enough to write in a journal, and so the serious reflectors, the ones with the dazzling follow-up questions, hardly ever went there.

Experienced Poohstickers know that in any forest game, the first, and most critical, task is collecting the proper sticks. As I had never seen any instructions for collecting proper sticks to replicate specific members of the communion of saints, I was a bit nervous as to how to proceed. But a Hum came to me soon enough—vaguely reminiscent of "Shall We Gather at the River"—and so I selected a few sticks and started to stand them in the circle I had drawn in the sand, one stick for each person who had helped me on the road toward God.

I began with the obvious ones—my parents, my brothers and sister, my children (*saints* is a relative term, is it not?), two pastors I had been close to, and my two best friends in the prayer community that was reflecting away all over the woods thereabouts. Then I put a stick in the ground for each of my grandparents, one for my best aunt/friend Bo, and then when I thought of aunts, I had to include Aunt Frances and Aunt Bertha. They were not actually my aunts; they were everybody's aunts. They taught Sunday school and greeted folks at the church where I grew up.

It came to me that if I were not more careful about height and weight and coloring for my sticks, I was going to lose track of who was in the group. And it was becoming clear that I was going to need a larger circle than I had first thought.

It also occurred me that if I was going to include Frances and Bertha, I should include those who used to take us on church retreats and such. So down went a stick for Henry and Billy and Wilson (tall stick, that one) and one each for the two Joes. Then two Betty sticks, and a Connie and a Judy.

Then I put in one each for the two schoolteachers who taught me to love books and writing, Mrs. Kirby and Ms. Flatt. It seemed to me that day that what they taught me has had as much to do with calling and the Word as it has with work and career. Once the literary arts entered the picture, it seemed only right to include Wordsworth and Frost and Buechner and Dillard and Milne and Greene and Gibran and Le Carré. Whatever this place is that I have wandered to on my journey, such writers helped bring me to it. They affected my journey toward God as surely as they affected my frequent journeys to the bookstore.

Then the faces of others, those whom I had loved and who had loved me, began to come into view—those who had held my hand and stolen my heart, those who had carried my burdens and lifted my spirits, those with whom I had worked and dreamed and sung and laughed and cried.

One of the things that struck me about my road to God that morning in the sand with my Saintsticks was that I had never not been on it. (I am sure that last is a double something; my apologies, Mrs. Kirby, wherever you are.) There were more than a few times when it seemed as though I was pretty lost in the woods, perhaps even in danger of heading toward a cliff without realizing it. But once I started toward God, I never really stopped and was never really in need of starting over.

Was I ever in need of confession and forgiveness and grace and a touch of providence itself? Certainly. Was I in need of turning toward God as though we were strangers to each other and had never met? No, not once. Which makes me no different from you, though it may well have taken me a lot longer to figure it out.

Once we start home toward God—which happens the minute we start, actually—we simply do not ever turn around and head in another direction. There is no other direction. And in the moments when we feel as if we are so turned around that we will never get home, somebody turns up and nudges us a couple of points to starboard, whichever direction that is. Suddenly, without being particularly conscious of it or faithful about it, we sense that we are headed toward God again full blast. Like a Pooh-stick that has finally stopped spinning around in an eddy or has escaped a log or a rock that was holding it back, we suddenly find ourselves slipping out from under the darkness beneath the bridge, into the light, heading for Home, the only place we have really been going.

You may well have known that and believed it all along, but I did not figure it out until I was kneeling in the sand over my Saintsticks that morning. And when I said it aloud to myself, with some considerable amount of wonder in my voice, the whole crowd of Saintsticks seemed to look up and grin and say, "Yes, yes, he finally got it." Then a hubbub seemed to come over them all, with lots of handshakes and slaps on the back and hugs all around. A general joy just sort of overtook all of us right then and there.

I began to see them then in their places, the places where they had been Christ to me—the hallways and the houses, the churches and the chapels, the schoolrooms and the shopping malls, the bars and the ball fields, the retreats and the restaurants. I saw them in doorways, opening their arms to me when I was hurting; on park benches, sharing their hope with me when I was afraid; in sanctuaries, throwing out lines to me when I was drowning.

I saw them walking beside me on roads I had walked thinking I was surely all alone, and I heard them laughing with me on golden days where the sun still shines even now. I saw them with their arms around me and their tears falling mixed with mine, in places so dark there was barely enough light for our tears to glisten.

I remembered those places, and then I knew what it meant to be on holy ground—ground that had been made holy by the One who made it and by those who walk it and do the work of the Christ on it. We do not often see the place we are standing as holy ground. But the fault does not lie with the ground; it lies with us. We do not always see the saints among us, either, but that is because we do not see what it is we are looking at.

We do not always see that we should be moving about our days and lives and places with awe and reverence and wonder, with the same soft steps with which we enter the room of a sleeping child or the mysterious silence of a cathedral. There is no ground that is not holy ground. All of the places of our lives are sanctuaries; some of them just happen to have steeples. And all of the people in our lives are saints; it is just that some of them have day jobs and most will never have feast days named for them.

❧

The Saintsticks count was up to about eighty when the portion of the community of saints that I have personally encountered was nearly kicked into the creek as a voice behind me said, "What are you doing?" Something about finding me kneeling in the sand humming a Pooh sort of version of the Doxology to a group of sticks standing in a circle seemed to have piqued someone's curiosity.

"Playing Saintsticks," I said as cheerfully and as normally as I could. There was a long pause.

"Oh."

I remember seeing the look I get from people when they see what I have come to call my holy-ground grin. It is the grin I get when someone catches me crying at yet another baptism of some kid I do not know or choking up whenever I hear the "Wesley Blessing" being sung by a crowd of church folks at a potluck supper or am standing transfixed by candlelit faces as we sing "O come, O come, Immanuel" at the winter solstice each year. It is the same look that I wear sometimes when I let my kids off at school and the big orange leaves from the giant oak in front of the old school chase them toward their day, or when I get a pat on the back at the watercooler and cannot get turned around fast enough to see who did it. Or when I read Philippians or Saint John or Psalm 139 or see *The Mission* or *The Postman* or read Buechner's autobiographies or Dillard's *The Writing Life*.

It is the look that always comes over me when I am paying enough attention to recognize that I am

standing on holy ground and have my eyes open for
saints that may be in the vicinity.

I paused for a minute or two that morning, waiting for my fellow reflector to decide that he would
go on back toward the class by himself, and quickly.
Whether he was very reverent or very nervous, I
could not tell. When I was alone again, I began to
walk out of the woods, very slowly, aware that each
next step was on holy ground. I worked out a little
Hum as I went, a Song for Reminding Myself to Walk
Slowly More Than I Used To.

No journey across holy ground should be rushed.

In three months I was back down for the week
with the community. I was still hungry, not holy yet,
the same way that I was the first time I went and that
I was the last time as well. The first thing I did was go
down to the creek to see if the Saintsticks were still
standing where I had last seen them.

They were not, of course. The winter rains had
come through the creek. The Saintsticks had moved
on, making other places into holy ground wherever
they had landed.

Which is, in the end, the object of the exercise: to become the saints we were dreamed into being to become.

The journey between the dreaming and the coming true is a journey made on holy ground. It is a journey made through silence and longing where, if we will listen, we can hear the whisper of the Dreamer echoing deep within us, calling us to become what the Dreamer sees when our names were first whispered: saints who believe in and pay attention for and recognize the Voice; saints who live our lives in joy and confidence and hope rather than judgment and anxiety and desperation; saints whose hours and days and lives are spent carrying people to the Christ, lending each other a hand when one of us has fallen, slipping along the river that brings joy to the heart of God, carrying God's peace and love and presence and life to those we meet along the way.

That is what we have been sent here to do. And we will. The Dreamer's dreams will always come true.